Recommended

Recommended

By J Christian Andersen

66 Success is built
of a series of
sometimes small
improvements.
Celebrate and
acknowledge
progress. **99**

Sue Glotfelty

Senior Director of Marketing Services, Cintas

RECOMMENDED

© 2015: J Christian Andersen,
Steven Henrik Jensen & Relationwise A/S

Relationwise A/S
info@relationwise.com
Phone.: (+45) 70 268 264

Cover art: Kiryl Lysenka, gnibel.com
Illustrations: Hugo Camacho, NowhereValley.com
Book design: Elena Carl, elenacarl.de
Published by: Motus

Forlag: BoD – Books on Demand, København, Danmark
Fremstilling: BoD - Books on Demand GmbH -
Norderstedt, Tyskland
ISBN: 9788771703696
First edition 2014

www.relationwise.com

Contents

Foreword

London, summer 2013

Dear reader,

A year ago I stumbled on an article from Bain & Company – one of the world's largest consultancy firms. The firm had created a new methodology that was producing fantastic results: the companies that were the pioneers of this new paradigm grew on average more than twice as fast as their competitors.

At a time when everyone is dreaming about growth, you can blame other factors for lack of success, or listen and wise up to what growth companies are doing right.

The genius of Bain & Company's methodology lies in its simplicity. In a simple yet highly effective way, businesses can grow by aiming at a single goal.

The goal is to gain more customers who are prepared to recommend the company to others.

At the same time, it is a very healthy learning process for employees. Everyone continually learns how to ensure that more and more customers are willing to recommend the company in the future. Simply put, this methodology puts an end to short-sighted goals and employees with self-satisfied overinflated privilege.

Instead, a corporate culture is created where all employees take responsibility for customer experience. This is a culture where customer service is not seen as an expense, but as an investment – and where the customer is a person treated with respect.

This book is the first step towards a better corporate culture.

At Relationwise, we would like to partner with other companies that want to grow by cultivating a corporate culture with a focus on the customer.

We hope that this book will inspire, and that we can share our experiences and help each other along the journey. This is why Part 2 is dedicated to the readers' own experiences.

I wish you luck!

Christian, partner at Relationwise A/S
Christian@relationwise.com, www.relationwise.com

Part 1

From Satisfied
to Recommended

1– Make your business a philosophy

A common goal

It's about time everyone in your company – you and your colleagues, management and the rest of the organisation, both back-office and frontline employees – had a common inspiring goal:

Find out how to make a difference so your customers will say:

"I like doing business with them."
"I'm going to choose them again next time" and
"I'm going to tell my friends and colleagues about them!"

Do your customers remember you? Are your customers takling about your company? Or are you just another one of those irrelevant suppliers customers do business with and then unceremoniously drop with the passing of time? Are you remembered at all?

The fight against fat-catism

If you adopt the philosophy you must do something for your customers instead of simply treating them like cash cows, you're already ahead. But all too often the focus is elsewhere. If things are going badly, it is often due to external situations. Then you can start blaming others. Of course, this is the easy way out; you are removing focus away from yourself. This is a part of what we call fat-cat-ism.

In Denmark, we actually have an official dictionary word for fat-catism: *selvfedme*. The closest we can get in English is the slang expression "fat cat", meaning a person who has become lazy or self-satisfied as the result of privilege or advantage. Sure, it might carry connotations of the arrogant city banker, but in our very important context of the theme of this book, it can mean anyone who takes an attitude of self-satisfied, overinflated privilege.

Being responsible for your customers

"Being responsible" doesn't just mean being more polite or baring a wider smile. It's all about taking responsibility for your customers.

You are here to make a difference. Instead of distancing yourself because you're always too busy hunting for new customers, you should focus on being responsible for and responsive to every single customer, both existing and potential.

It's about time businesses injected a human perspective into their operations, rather than following a short-sighted and clinical approach. It's about time we rediscovered the fundamental value of loyalty.

This is not a CSR strategy. This is an attempt to make the lives of our customers a little bit better.

This way of thinking can really pay dividends, but more about that later.

A mission statement and internally distributed newsletter are not enough. This approach demands full focus and engagement by the entire company – including those who don't have direct customer contact. As we will discover later in this book, the galvanisation of employees and transformation of the entire corporate culture are the keys to creating a great business.

When loyalty is misunderstood

Why should you even be bothered about customer loyalty? Companies today are increasingly faced with a fundamental challenge: lack of customers.

Many businesses are finding they are not growing in the same way as they used to, and there are now considerable challenges to gaining new customers. Every company that has done the calculation knows it is far more economical to retain existing customers than gain new ones.

But many businesses appear to have a problem even understanding what customer loyalty actually involves. Customer loyalty is often approached one-dimensionally: businesses expect customers to be loyal to them, yet they themselves are not loyal to their customers. A good example is a newspaper subscription. As a loyal customer to a particular newspaper for a number of years, you learn one day that your neighbour (who previously subscribed to a different newspaper) has switched to the same one as you – and is only paying a third of the price you're paying! Why are new customers rewarded but not loyal ones? From the newspaper's perspective, it has gained a new customer – but he is not loyal: in other words, it is economically sound in the short term, but will hurt the business in the long term.

Maintaining the hunger

Rasmus Ankersen, an author and international speaker, has written a couple of books, one of which is entitled *Leader DNA*. In this book, he writes about how businesses and employees can perform better. His focus is predominantly on the world of sport; he has travelled around the world and, among other things, decoded why they are so good at golf in South Korea and why so many of the world's best runners come from the same little village in Ethiopia. Some very interesting stories have emerged from his research.

Rasmus was visiting Nokia in Finland. When the iPhone started taking over the market, their CEO said, "The iPhone will always be a niche product." He firmly believed Apple would never become a real competitor and Nokia would retain their dominant position in the market.

They were smitten with fat-catism. The entire company was patting themselves on the backs and proclaiming they were the best in the world and nobody could topple them. They were too busy focusing on what was happening within their own four walls and completely forgot to look at what was happening in the market and with the customers. It seems obvious that you should listen to your customers – yet many businesses are so into fat-catism that, as Rasmus Ankersen explains, "They lose their hunger."

When Lars Løkke Rasmussen (former Danish Prime Minister) wrote his book *The Danish Dream*, Rasmus Ankersen contributed a chapter entitled "How to create hunger in paradise." When things are going really well, how do you keep your drive and your hunger alive? And from a business's perspective, how can it move its focus from itself to its customers?

This is done by constantly asking customers: "What can we do better?" Not just whether or not they are satisfied, but asking them what it would take for them to have a "wow experience."

Sometimes you just want to shout, "Listen to your customer, damn it! Listen to what they're saying." It is this that should be driving your business. It isn't about approaching the customer with an attitude of self-satisfied arrogance. You shouldn't treat your customers in a conveyor-belt-like fashion. You must fight for every customer you get, and give the best of yourself every time. There is no longer a place for businesses that are only chugging along at half steam.

Old-school customer satisfaction surveys lead to laziness

Something that is common for many businesses affected by fat-catism is that they use inappropriate analysis methods. The classic mistake is to measure using the five-scale rating method (Very dissatisfied – Dissatisfied – Neither satisfied nor dissatisfied – Satisfied – Very satisfied). Many companies tend to lump the categories of "Satisfied" and "Very satisfied" together and claim (for example) a ninety-five per cent customer satisfaction rate.

But there's a big difference between being satisfied and being very satisfied – and just because customers answered "satisfied" (or even "very satisfied") that doesn't mean they are loyal customers. No: customers need to have had the "wow experience" meaning that they've been really impressed by something the company has done and it has exceeded their expectations. The alternative, from the company's perspective, is simply the cultivation of laziness with the only goal seeming to be the preservation of the status quo.

It is all about the culture

Customer loyalty is all about corporate culture. There is a tendency in companies today, especially international businesses, towards a culture of arrogance. Many businesses sorely need a wake-up call in this regard.

If you maintain the myth you have reached the top (and you believe you can stay there without daily hard work), inertia becomes a goal in itself. But the world doesn't stand still, and neither do the needs of customers.

Imagine you're a butcher in a supermarket. Early one morning, before the supermarket opens for customers, you decide to take a walk through the various departments as your colleagues are stacking their shelves with goods. In the grocery corner you see that the greengrocer has built an amazing pyramid of tomatoes. You notice that a single tomato at the top is rotten. Here, you can choose to do one of two things: take the tomato and gently explain to the greengrocer that such a prominent rotten tomato could damage the supermarket's overall reputation for freshness, or continue on to your colleagues in the butchers' department and poke fun at the incompetent greengrocer. This story illustrates why corporate culture is so important.

Another example: you are having a meeting in an open office space. In the space adjacent to you, the phone is ringing constantly and the guy you're speaking to says, "It's typical; Smith has forgotten to forward his calls again." Why is he complaining? Pick up Smith's phone and take the call – it could be a customer!

A good sign that a company is customer-orientated can be found in the car park. A customer-orientated company will tend to have customer parking spaces located close to the entrance. In the product-orientated business, its management's cars are right bang by the entrance. It says a lot about the corporate culture. It is the same when you enter the reception area; you quickly get a feel for whether you are truly welcome or you are just taking up their time.

Change begins for those who dare

Sometimes it is because you have a boardroom that is put together in the wrong way. It is often occupied by lawyers and accountants whose gaze is too firmly fixed on the rear-view mirror, making them cautious and mistrusting. It is crucial that at this level you have someone who is representing and gunning for the customers.

Businesses need more diversity and edge. It is a common challenge for many businesses. They simply do not have enough edge. Many employees are so obsessed about making a career for themselves, and so afraid of making mistakes, that in reality they end up doing little more than irrelevant maintenance – which will not drive a business. What is really needed are employees who are prepared to express and fight for their opinions. We often lack these types of employee profiles. We have altogether too many smooth, nice, boring types.

Everyone talks about change because it sounds good. But to actually put actions behind those words is an entirely different matter, because then suddenly you're responsible for those bold actions and are no longer able to blame others if customers start abandoning the company. Who hasn't tried to blame (for example) unfair price competition, the financial crisis and everything else under the sun? Change happens when you start taking a critical look at yourself. But many have become so comfortable they don't even bother listening to customers – that's too much like hard work as then you will actually have to do something they request. It is a lot easier to just stick to your own little agenda so you can go home at five o'clock.

“ Many employees are so obsessed about making a career for themselves and so afraid of making mistakes, that in reality they end up doing little more than irrelevant maintenance – which simply will not drive a business. **”**

The Rockefeller Institute compiles "TARP studies" each year, with analyses of why customers abandon companies. From that research, it has been revealed that only nine per cent of customers say that it is because of the actual price. And the major reason? Sixty-eight per cent of customers said that bad communication and service were the predominant reasons they were prompted to look elsewhere. This is rock-solid proof of the importance of communication with customers and working actively to improve customer loyalty.

Do you create change? Or are you, in reality, suppressing it? Get out in front and be the person in the company who starts the change. You will be rewarded.

Summary

- Make pleasing customers the inspiring goal that ignites a flame and energises your employees.
- The goal is not satisfied customers. Satisfied is the same as mediocre.
- Create a culture in which employees continually develop and improve.

Customer service in Silicon Valley

On a visit to San Francisco, I stopped by a café called Coupa Café in Palo Alto. After ten minutes, I still hadn't got the cup of coffee I'd ordered, so I asked one of the employees for it. Five minutes later, still nothing, so I asked again, only to be told it was on its way. It was a further five minutes before I got my coffee, and by that time my patience had worn thin.

So I wrote on their Facebook wall that surely having to wait twenty minutes for a coffee was something they could improve on. After just a couple of hours they answered:

I'm sorry for the delay. We are short-staffed, but we will be back to normal tomorrow. Thank you!

It is great that they answered after just a couple of hours – indeed, it is a better response rate than that of many of the IT corporations dotted throughout Silicon Valley. So far so good. But if they had actually recognised good service as an investment instead of an expense, they might have written something like this:

"We apologise for the delay. Drop by again and get a cup of coffee on the house – and this time with fast service."

The cost of the coffee would have been minimal. I might even have bought something to complement the coffee and they would have made a profit from my visit. And that experience might have made me into a loyal customer who would have recommended them to others.

The question you ought to ask yourself today is: Does everyone in your company know that good service is not an expense but actually an investment?

2 – A new goal

Most companies have already made inspiring mission statements and shown good intentions. But a mission without the possibility to measure results usually just remains hot air.

Net Promoter Score

It's important to implement methodology that ensures good intentions can be measured, providing you with an ongoing gauge of where you're at. In this way, you can make course corrections in the case of less than satisfactory results. It isn't a coincidence that some of the world's most successful companies, such as Apple, for example, use systematic customer measurement principles. And they don't use just any system. They use the Net Promoter Score® (NPS)*. This is the methodology we recommend too. We are not getting anything from recommending it; we are doing it for the very simplest

* Net Promoter, NPS, and Net Promoter Score are trademarks of Satmetrix Systems, Inc., Bain & Company, and Fred Reichheld. It is an open system available to all.

of reasons – that it is the best system. Extremely simple to implement, analyse and act upon, NPS provides you with a score that is directly comparable to benchmark, both internally between different departments and employees, but also externally against competitors and other sectors.

NPS was founded and introduced by the acclaimed consultancy firm Bain & Company together with Fred Reichheld. It is readily available to anyone who wishes to use it.

It all started back in 2003 when Fred Reichheld (who was also employed by Harvard) conducted extensive research to discover what would be the best question to ask customers in order to get an indication and a direct correlation to company growth. They researched a myriad of different questions, and the "recommended" question proved to be the one with the strongest correlation with a company's profit margins – and in particular the link between increased purchasing behaviour and willingness to recommend the brand to others. The more willing a customer was to recommend the brand, the more willing he/she would be to purchase the product him/herself.

The other strong correlation was "word of mouth." Not surprisingly, it was "word of mouth" recommendations to friends and colleagues that resulted in increased sales.

In 2006, Fred Reichheld published his book *The Ultimate Question*, which today is widely regarded as the bible of NPS.

The implementation of NPS has been extensive throughout the USA and is growing in the UK.

A KPI that can predict the future

NPS can do something no other methodology can. Imagine you have a KPI that shows what will happen in the future. You have plenty of KPIs indicating what the current or past situation is, but it is uncommon for companies to have a KPI that predicts how their customers will behave in the future. This is the fantastic thing about NPS – it manages to do just this.

What about the classic satisfaction scores? When you ask a customer to tell you about his/her customer experience or satisfaction, what you are actually asking them to do is tell you about the past. But you don't ask them to tell you whether they'll come again, and certainly not whether they're so happy about the product or service that they'd actually tell other people about it.

" The distinction between loyalty and satisfaction is essentially that satisfaction is something that has already happened. Loyalty is all about expected future behaviour. **"**

The research that inspired the methodology showed that the question that best reflected customer loyalty and future behaviour was:

How likely are you to recommend us to others?

The customer is requested to respond to this question on a scale going from 0 (not likely at all) to 10 (extremely likely).
The customer is then asked to leave a few comments:

What could we improve?

This question is added because it is also important to understand the reason for dissatisfaction and what could be improved. What are the factors that are driving customer loyalty and the promoters?

If in the first question the customer answers 9-10, they are genuinely loyal customers, and we call them "promoters".

Scores of 7-8 in classic customer satisfaction analysis would be considered a satisfied customer, but in this system they are rated as passive satisfied. They are not yet at a level where they have a strong enough connection that they would be prepared to pro-actively recommend you. A customer who gives you a score of 7-8 could therefore choose a competitor next time round if they feel they have good reason (for example, a good special offer or great word of mouth from your competitors' promoters).

If a customer scores you from 0-6, they are certainly not loyal to your brand and are therefore considered to be "detractors". These customers may choose to leave at any time. Furthermore, if they score you from 0-4, there is a considerable risk that they will spread negative word of mouth about your business.

NPS can be found by subtracting the detractors (0-6) from the promoters (9-19). For example, a business might have the following results:

Promoters	55 per cent
Passives	25 per cent
Detractors	20 per cent

This will result in an NPS score of 35 (55-20).
An example of a company with a very impressive

NPS is Apple which has a stable score of approximately seventy-two per cent. If your company can achieve anywhere near this score, the future looks very bright. Although it may sound absurd to compare your company to Apple, you have to remember that with the techniques described in this book, it is certainly not unrealistic to reach a comparable level in terms of customer loyalty.

Overall, NPS is split into three categories:

(-100) – 0:	Bad
0 – 50:	Mediocre
50-100:	Great

There has been much debate about whether it is more effective to measure the results of customer research on a 5- or 10-point scale. We strongly recommend the 10-point scale. It's the easiest for customers to relate to and provides a more nuanced picture of the results. And, most importantly, it is the 10-point scale that NPS builds on, so you won't have to perform recalculations that will make comparisons with other NPS companies less valid.

How likely are you to recommend us to others?

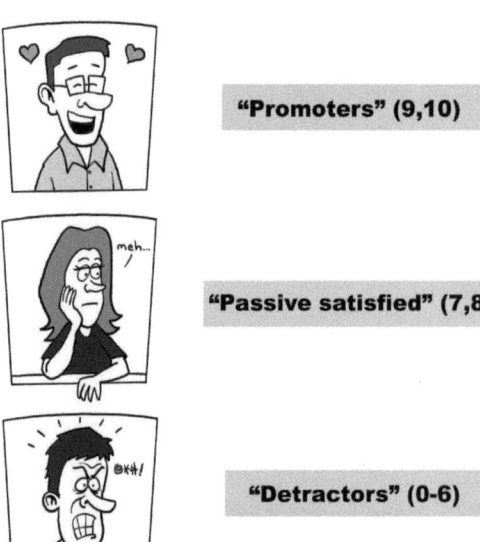

"Promoters" (9,10)

"Passive satisfied" (7,8)

"Detractors" (0-6)

Measure it on the bottom line

It goes without saying that when measurements are being taken we should also measure results on the bottom line.

Let's make a simple calculation that illustrates the lifetime value of a customer: At Relationwise we have had countless meetings with sales and marketing directors who had not yet done the very important calculation that shows what they stand to lose in terms of pounds and pennies if customer retention is low. In the event you have not done the maths, the following is a quick guide.

Of course, for some companies it is going to be challenging to make an exact calculation because it is often difficult to measure exactly how many customers come and go, which are regular customers, and which buy in what quantity. Nevertheless, it is always preferable to have an estimated calculation rather than nothing at all.

Here is an example of the calculation in its simplest form: On average, ten per cent of company ABC's customers do not recommit after the first year's purchase. On average, every purchase is worth ten euros. If

ABC has 500 customers, this means that fifty of their customers will not give the potential income of ten thousand each in the next year. This gives an accumulated loss of five hundred thousand euros on potential income.

But that's just the first year. Over five years, those five hundred thousand euros become two point five million euros, and after ten years they become five million euros. If ABC had managed to retain just a fraction of their lost customers, they would be at least hundreds of thousands of euros richer.

While it's true that ABC loses ten per cent of their customers each year, they also gain ten per cent more new customers. The company therefore manages just fine, and it isn't overly concerned by its lost customers. But just because you gain new customers, it doesn't justify losing customers at the other end. If ABC halved its defections, it would achieve a five per cent growth rate instead of being stuck in the status quo as competitors jump ahead. And we shouldn't forget the expenses associated with winning the ten per cent more new customers.

You could dig even deeper and link the loyalty score with other numbers found in your CRM (Customer Relationship Management) and commerce systems. There are huge opportunities in this data that companies rarely tap into. Suddenly, you have answers to these kinds of questions:

- What economic influence does a detractor and a promoter have?
- How long, on average, do detractors and promoters remain customers?
- What is the life value of detractors (even negative value) and promoters respectively?
- What will it mean (economically) to strive to convert a share of your detractors to promoters?
- If you can create change based on the facts listed in the box, what financial gain could you achieve?

Customer loyalty also affects the bottom line in a way that's often overlooked.

The US Office of Consumer Affairs has for years highlighted the correlation between the way a complaint is managed by a company and the subsequent decision of the dissatisfied customer as to whether or not to purchase from that company again. It has been proven that seventy-five to ninety-five per cent of dissatisfied customers never complain!

It has also been proven that the time between the complaints to the time that the company either reacts or solves the problem has a direct influence on the probability that the customer will choose to stay with the company.

The percentage of customers with "big complaints" that remain customers rises from nine to nineteen per cent simply because they have submitted their complaint – even if the complaint has not yet been solved. If the company solves the problem, then customer retention rises to fifty-four per cent – and if the problem is solved speedily, then it rises to a whopping eighty-two per cent!

In other words, change your "win-back" from nine percent to eighty-two per cent.

What financial impact would this have on your company?

Promoters and the effect they have on your business

How many of your customers currently purchase from you based on a recommendation from another customer?

The number of customers generated from a recommendation will be different depending on the market segment. Peter Winther from Winholistic established an estimate after researching a series of Danish companies. His research shows that (depending on the market) if a single promoter recommends a company to just four other people, there is a high possibility that one of them will end up becoming a customer.

According to the "formula" above, you need forty recommendations to obtain approximately ten new customers.

Of course, we need to make the distinction between a Facebook like and a real recommendation to someone we know well. How many new customers can be accredited to promoter recommendations depends on how good we are at activating our promoters to recommend our company.

All this is supported by the fact that we are much more inclined to trust a recommendation from our friends and acquaintances than we are to believe in corporate promises or expert advice.

If you could double the amount of your promoters, those that rated you 9 or 10, how many customers would you be able to get?

Even with conservative estimates, you will probably discover that there are big gains to be made (directly affecting the bottom line) by working with customer loyalty.

Listen to your customers and find out what it takes to convert them into promoters. According to Tomas Lykke Nielsen, the author behind the critically acclaimed *Take Responsibility for the Customer*, there are some commonalities. He says:

"There is a phenomenon that is particularly clear. Companies that have many promoters have a high frequency of communication with their customers. They inform their customers when there is something relevant for the customer to know. They pro-actively suggest improvements to the customers' products, they inform customers when they've made an error, and they keep customers constantly up to date when the customers are involved in processes (what's happening now, how far are we, etc.). We propose that one of the fastest ways to get more promoters is to step up the customer communication – as long as it's relevant, because it strengthens and maintains the relationship with the customer."

Mobilise your ambassadors and create your own movement

So far so good – but how do you take the next step? How do you mobilise your ambassadors to ensure your great product or message goes viral? Well, first of all you need to find out how your company can make the world a better place. You need to work out how you can get your customers to love you and tell the story of that - but it is important to have the right foundations first. You can't expect your ambassadors to help you create a movement before your company is able to provide excellent customer experiences and until your company has a Net Promoter Score of a minimum of 50. Customer loyalty is the condition to get them to share your vision and spread the word.

Think big and share your vision with your customers. In order to start a movement you need to pinpoint the vision that you share with your customers.

You need to make your starting point your honest values; from here, you will be able to find the vision that builds a bridge between your company, your customers and the world you meet each other in.

Recommend. Finding a joint vision requires awareness of your own values and in-depth knowledge of your customers. You need to start a dialogue with your customers and get to know them better. Think big. The vision needs to be worth talking about. If you don't think big enough, your customers won't be talking about you.

You can now get your customers involved. Your and your ambassadors' vision should now be shared with the world. One of the best ways to share your vision and start a movement is through personal stories. We know this from Steve Jobs' legendary product presentations where his message to his followers was always to challenge the status quo. Another example is the bank Itaú in São Paulo which developed a value-based marketing campaign by sponsoring a network of city bikes, creating a cycling culture that didn't exist before. Several other companies are inspiring and educating millions of people on a daily basis by publishing their own books and giving them away for free on the Internet – helping others while simultaneously creating a movement that the company benefits from.

Is it easy to start a movement? No, it's not. I would say that only a few take the plunge and seriously start mobilising their ambassadors in order to start a movement. It is of course much easier to call your PR company and get them to come up with a campaign with glossy photos – but commercials and ads will probably not change the world. Customers sense this and therefore the campaign's effect on your sales will be short-lived or perhaps won't have any impact at all.

Summary

- Find out how much money your company is losing as a result of lost "lifetime" customers.
- Find out how many of your customers are truly loyal and would be prepared to recommend you to others.
- Find those customers who are potentially less likely to be loyal and enter into dialogue with them.

Lessons from LEGO Group

Your smartest people don't work in your company.

Conny Kalcher, Vice President of Marketing and Consumer Experiences at LEGO, recalls how one of their adult fans became so angry that he actually contacted the owner of LEGO Group, Kjeld Kirk, and their CEO, Jørgen Vig Knudstorp. The customer asked how LEGO could be so indifferent to the fact that he had cancelled an order, and why hadn't they even asked him why he had cancelled?

That was an eye opener for LEGO Group. Today LEGO Group involves their customers much more. Customers are being listened to and the quality of their experiences at the various LEGO touchpoints are being measured.

LEGO Group is today such a showcase example that they are referenced again and again by the founder of NPS, Fred Reichheld, in his book *The Ultimate Question 2.0*.

The LEGO Group is also working intensively to engage their many adult LEGO fans (AFOLS's). They have even developed a special ambassador program with 105 ambassadors in 35 counties, each with their own LEGO User Groups (LUGS) representing more than 200.000 members.

Conny Kalcher continues: *"Our consumer focus has become much sharper as a part of the turnaround we had. As it turns out, we weren't good enough at understanding our consumers in that period, so we pursued our own strategic plans, without listening to the children.*

It has certainly been a part of our turnaround story, that we are currently far more outside-in today than we've ever been. There were some very distinct buttons we had to turn to create that transformation. A consumer perspective also helps to create change internally in the company: making something excellent for the consumer is a great beacon to navigate towards. So when you are in a process of change, it is a really great thing to bring into the game.

Our founder, Ole Kirk Christiansen, was always very customer-orientated. It's part of our inheritance. He said, 'Only the best is good enough.' When he introduced it, he knew that if we made high-quality toys, then the consumer would spread the word and this in turn would become our marketing machine. We also believe that the only way to create growth and success is by understanding the consumers on a deep level, and delivering what they ask for.

We lost our way during the economic crisis. We believed our brand was strong enough to save us. We lost focus of our consumers' core needs: what five- to nine-year-old. boys want, and then what the girls wanted, to have a good experience. During the crisis, we spent a lot of energy getting back to what is the core experience that they want, and how can we deliver it and constantly improve it. This has been the path to success for us during our turnaround process.

Another challenge was that we had simply become too large for our own good and were no longer able to clearly see where we were creating value and where we were not creating value. We went in too many different directions because we forgot that we have a core, our bread and butter, that we must never lose focus of. We can do other things around that core, but if we lose the core, then we can no longer create growth."

3 – Change management

What will it take for your employees to start working on customer loyalty towards achieving that perfect 10?

Mirror mirror on the wall...

It's our experience that the challenge in working with customer loyalty is not just about getting individual employees to focus more on customer loyalty; the challenge is mostly with senior management. They are the ones who need to set an example. It takes courage to look at yourself in the "loyalty mirror" every day, constantly being measured to gauge whether it's getting better or worse. The kind of proactivity required in order to focus on constant improvement is what separates mediocre senior management from the best – those who constantly move onward and upward.

This means that the company needs to re-prioritise customer surveys, ensuring they are carried out consistently on a daily basis rather than just annually.

Perhaps this sounds expensive. Perhaps it is. But it would be far more expensive to not do it.

You must stop seeing dissatisfied customers as just a percentage/statistic. If a friend of yours approached you with a serious problem, would you ignore him/her or discard it at the bottom of a to-do list? No, you would deal with it immediately. This is how you need to start treating your customers. It is all about treating each other as fellow human beings. And from a business point of view, this approach really pays dividends.

You need to start contacting every single dissatisfied customer and turn them into a satisfied one, or perhaps even convert them into promoters. But this all starts with involving the entire organisation, from top to bottom, and everyone needs to feel that they are an integral part of the endeavour. When individuals feel a sense of ownership, their involvement and investment will be much greater.

Put customer loyalty on the agenda at management meetings. Not much will change if customer loyalty is delegated to a small group of enthusiasts – a small island in a big ocean of an organisation. A CEO needs to sit at the end of the table and customer feedback needs to be read out aloud. Reading out comments from both dissatisfied and satisfied customers often has a greater impact and influence than simply looking at a statistic sent from head office once a month/every six months.

Based on the customer feedback, an action plan should be developed. This is one of the reasons a CEO needs to be at one end of the table, because then the process of change has real weight behind it. It will be much more effective.

The action plan must be operational. If the goal, for example, is an NPS of 80, what operational targets (such as allocation of time for correcting errors) should

the company strive for? This is where the battle is fought to understand the connection between operational data and customer experience.

The action plan must be communicated to all relevant employees, and a system must be established to ensure that feedback from dissatisfied customers is dealt with in real time. If the employee is confronted with problems as they occur, and is simultaneously reminded of what they are doing well and what they need to improve, then they have the opportunity to mend fences and build on their strengths to both the customers' and the employees' satisfaction.

As an executive, you should also have an overview of how each employee is performing. You can easily identify who isn't doing well relative to the level of customer loyalty. As such, you will know how to allocate your resources. You can reward the high performers and guide the low performers towards improvement, with insights into exactly what is going wrong. The entire organisation and every individual employee is now united in moving the company closer to that score of 10.

In the case of a dissatisfied customer, the employee himself should receive the complaint so he is able to take action pro-actively. The employee should also be able to see how customer loyalty develops over time so the improvements the employee is working on can be observed in the form of increased customer loyalty. And, of course, as an executive or manager, you should identify when individuals make solid improvements so you can give them the recognition they deserve. This will become a positive feedback loop which motivates them to continue to do even better.

It is here that we see the crucial significance of working with customer loyalty in a systematic way: the real value is the cultural change that gradually occurs in which every single employee starts to make individual improvements on a daily basis. Ultimately, it is not about the technique but the habits – the good habits.

Depending on the organisation and how motivated they are to change, the processes can be implemented gradually,with a matching level of ambition.

Start by involving only those employees who have direct frontline customer contact. They might have the directive to always follow up on dissatisfied customers within forty-eight hours. Eventually, this could be reduced to twenty-four hours. By comparison, successful companies such as Apple aim to answer dissatisfied customers within twenty-four hours – an aim they fulfil in ninety per cent of cases.

Employee involvement

You can formulate an excellent job description, but if the incentive structure creates behaviour that results in a different outcome to what the job description intended, that is what they'll aim for. Perhaps there are some employees who are not particularly interested in going the extra mile for the customer because they will not be rewarded for it. They can hide away in the organisation – especially in larger corporations. That is why there should be an emphasis on customer loyalty even during

 Apple is among the best in the world when it comes to customer loyalty. Many believe that this loyalty stems primarily from its fantastic products or design, but it has been proven that the most important factor for their promoters is the way employees in the Apple stores treat them. Employees discuss customer feedback as a part of their daily routine. This kind of corporate culture has produced very significant results. From an NPS score of 58 when they started measuring in 2007, it had risen all the way up to 72 in 2012.

the recruitment process. Find employees who already have the correct mindset to make a difference.

But what do you do about the employees who already have some of that fat-catism? How does the manager engage them? McKinsey has discovered what they call the "meaning quotient". In the same sense that we have an IQ and EQ (emotional intelligence), we also have an MQ. We all know that a high IQ and EQ are necessary among employees to enable them to perform at a high level, but if an employee has a deficit MQ (not enough meaning behind what the employee is doing), he will not perform to his full potential.

Fascinating new research has shown what motivates employees – and it is no longer the salary that takes centre stage, despite the fact that many companies are still very old school in this area. Of course, salaries should be paid, but beyond that it's a bad incentive model. "Meaningfulness" is essential. This is why a focus on the customers and making a difference for them is a motivating goal for an employee. McKinsey uses, among others, Emerson Electric (a US Fortune 500 company) as a case study. Their CEO, David Farr, is known for asking all employees the following four questions:

1. How do you make a difference? (meaning)
2. What are you currently working to actively improve? (constant improvement)
3. When did you last receive coaching from your manager? (personal development)
4. Who is our biggest competitor? (creates solidarity)

All four questions ensure that the employee feels meaning, makes constant improvements and feels commonality with his colleagues.

Find out what motivates your employees. But start by investigating how they are managing in relation to customer loyalty. Don't judge them by how nice they are as a colleague. Instead, allow your customers to be the judge. Those who do least well are also those who are least motivated – and you should focus your attention on them.

At this point, I would like to give you a warning. Do you remember the example earlier in the book about the butcher who felt he was not affected by the greengrocer's success and was therefore unwilling to help him? We need to develop a corporate culture that is fully focused on our common humanity and going above and beyond the call of duty for both customers and colleagues.

For example, when a sales manager talks to his employees, he can have a more constructive dialogue because he can focus on the issues that matter and can identify where the necessity of both optimisation and reward should be placed.

Sales employees often have their own agenda. Of first and foremost concern is covering your own backside. So if you suspect dissatisfaction among a certain salesman's customers, it is important to back it up with solid facts, and at the same time try to foster a corporate culture that promotes solidarity and one within which everyone helps everyone else to make a difference.

Bolia.com

An example of a company that has implemented a system that produces natural employee participation is the furniture design group Bolia.com. Bolia.com has many stores in many countries, and therefore has the need to benchmark performance and customer feedback between its international stores. Bolia.com has developed a real-time customer feedback system that provides an international view of performance for the entire group and within each store. Customers also have the opportunity to provide direct written feedback and ideas for the Bolia concept, the collections, and each store and sales representative. This encourages strong customer and employee incentives for participation to improve the stores and performance. At the top level, weekly follow-ups are made based on the results. Negative feedback is quickly collected by a central team and the customer is contacted with the intention of converting them from a detractor to a promoter. At Bolia.com, all strategic business plans are developed with a focus squarely on the customer, and this culture has produced record sales several years in a row.

What makes the difference?

Investment will need to be made financially, emotionally and timewise for the NPS programme to function optimally. It is necessary to reduce the distance to the customer to achieve change in the score and in customer experience.

Neil Berkett is the chief executive at Virgin Media. When they introduced their NPS in 2006, there was a number of things they immediately needed to improve. Neil said, "It really doesn't help to force the programme down the throats of the employees. They all need to believe in the concept behind NPS. It's necessary to convince them – and this is a management responsibility –that this is something that can help the individual. Where they are keen to make the change because they see it helping themselves, their colleagues and the entire company. It was the task of selling the NPS programme to the frontline staff and really getting them to believe that this was something that they should believe in, that was difficult."

Virgin Media decided that the NPS was the best way to create a cultural change in the frontline. They had just completed a merger with Telewest and NTL, and had therefore inherited a frontline delivery capacity that was below par. And with the new Virgin brand, they also needed to somehow change the experience that was being delivered to customers, through customer service and through touchpoints (contact with customers) in the business. And NPS was seen as a motivation to bring about this cultural change.

A template for success

Initially, it's essential that top management are brought into the programme. It isn't something you just agree on and say, "Yes, okay, NPS is the right step forward." Management must be a part of the decision-making process in relation to how one must act. Of course, we're not talking about routine decisions that are taken every single day, but abut key structural improvements.

The results should be routed to the frontline. You need insight into the knowhow that is in the frontline because these are the employees who actually create change.

It is also important to produce proof as you move through the programme in order to maintain acceptance by those who still doubt the value of NPS – create the proof because there is no doubt that this proof is important in the company.

And the whole thing needs to be kept together by a professional team that can implement best practices, monitor internal communication, create guidelines, and say, "Okay, guys. It's a scale between 0 and 10. Promoters are 9s or 10s." The team must ensure good management regarding what is right and wrong in relation to rolling out the programme.

But the programme also requires delegation to establish exactly who is responsible for closing the loop on the customer. Make it clear. Have the process designed upfront before the surveys are sent. It is important that the programme is centrally coordinated and that you have a core team that can relate to all the business functions and areas because everyone has an interest in customer experience – not just the research department. This is relevant across the entire company.

If you want to go one step further, integrate it with your CRM system. See customer feedback directly together with all the other information about your customers. This will enable you to obtain the big picture about a single customer. It is great to get feedback and then say, "How can I help you with your problem?" But it is even better if you can see the information together with which products they use, where they live, etc.

Summary

- Put customer loyalty on the agenda. Make it a daily habit.
- Make a strategy for involving employees.
- Start the process today and start small. Success often builds on a series of small improvements. You might start with customer feedback readings at your next management meeting.

 The CEO at Zappos says what made the difference to his business was when they began to define the culture. They developed ten company values – not just a nice list to hang in a pretty picture frame, which employees would not have the motivation to comply with. They really delved into how to get employees to comply with the new corporate culture. The following is a good example:

Some employees of Zappos were visiting one of their partner companies. After the meeting they had a couple of beers, got slightly drunk and were on their way back to the hotel. One of the employees from the partner company had really been looking forward to a pizza back at the hotel, but when they returned they were told it was too late. They no longer served pizza at that hour. The woman was really down about it. So one of the Zappos te am said she should try and call Zappos, because they always offered fantastic customer service. It was said as a joke – they were, after all, slightly drunk – but the woman thought, "Okay, if you offer such good service, then I'm going to call right now." Zappos has 24/7 support, so she called them right then and there.

"Hello, I would like to order a pizza." There was silence and then the support rep told her diplomatically, "You do know we sell shoes – right?"

"Yes, I know that, but I was told that Zappos offer a fantastic service, so I would like a pizza. I'm down on Venice Beach, and it's one o'clock in the morning."

Now there was even more silence at the other end of the line. "Give me a moment," she was told.

A couple of minutes passed and then she was told, "I've found three pizza restaurants in your area that are still open. The addresses are…"

It would be impossible to define guidelines to anticipate what to do if customers call and ask for something out of the ordinary such as a pizza. You can only provide fantastic service if it is part of the culture. It all depends on making a strong corporate culture. Just like a society that has good culture, good values, ethics – a company needs these things too.

4 – Companies undergoing change

 **DANHOSTEL**

Most of the Danhostel group of 95 hostels work to strengthen their customer loyalty. This has given great results in a strongly competitive hotel and overnight accommodation market. Up to 25 per cent of customers return to stay with Danhostel.

How does Danhostel achieve these results? And how can their story inspire you to improve customer loyalty in your own company?

Danhostel conducts regular evaluations of what guests think about their stay. The main purpose of the evaluations is to improve the guests' experiences.

Danhostel obtains the ratings upon the guest's departure from the hostel – this is customary in the accommodation industry. Guests are given an evaluation survey to fill in. The employees in the individual hostels can then see for themselves what the guests have said and how they have rated their stay at the hostel.

In some hostels, evaluations are used extensively. Guest evaluations, for example, are reviewed every week during staff meetings. At this point, the management are able to say, for example, "We can see that guest satisfaction with cleanliness could be improved." This enables the hostel to set goals for guest satisfaction in terms of cleanliness. The guest evaluations give staff the opportunity to see how they themselves can make an impact on improving the hostel's rating. This approach has been a great success in several of the group's hostels in Copenhagen.

Danhostel completes a guest evaluation once a week. These periodic assessments are undoubtedly the reason that they have managed to strengthen their corporate culture.

In a large national organisation like Danhostel, it can be a challenge to get everyone to work with guest evaluations. Danhostel therefore assembles all of the group's nationwide staff once a year to discuss best practices. During the meeting, select members present their approaches to using the guest evaluations. Additionally, Danhostel uses the quality assurance programme HighQ from the group's international organisation. Many of the group's hostels are in the process of implementing this programme.

Every year, Danhostel employees nominate the year's best hosts. The criteria for being chosen as the year's best host is that the hosts and their employees have shown great innovation and resolve to help other hostels.

Danhostel is currently considering allowing customers to choose the year's best host. Throughout the whole organisation, work is ongoing to present stories about the hostels that have done particularly well during the year.

In the future, guest evaluations will play a major part in Danhostel's efforts to improve customer loyalty. Their ambition is that there should always be a balance between price and quality.

In previous years, guest evaluations were stored in an internal system, but today the evaluations have a central position on Danhostel's home page where they are visible to the entire Internet.

The individual hostels can respond to negative evaluations – this was one of the conditions Danhostel set when choosing the system. This means that a hostel can only be evaluated by a person who has actually stayed there. It also enables the hostel to contact the customer who had a bad experience, which is consistent with the group's concept.

Individual hostels can compile all the reports from the system that they might need. Each hostel can see their own position relative to similar hostels, and how satisfied the guests are according to the various evaluation criteria.

Consequently, Danhostel avoids the need for customer satisfaction efforts to be top-down managed. At the same time, employees feel that the system makes a positive difference to their day-to-day work, which is crucial to ensuring follow-up is carried out on negative evaluations. In addition, the fact that hostels can benchmark themselves against each other increases employee motivation.

Danhostel's experience demonstrates how effective such an approach is at the national level when representatives for the various hostels promote the systems implemented.

If this does not happen, employees will inevitably feel that management has too many requirements and wants to implement too many systems.

The evaluation system puts ratings centre-stage, whereas the star classification system was previously the main focus. Positive ratings can result in guests who previously would not have considered accommodation in a three-star hostel changing their minds.

The group still fights against a public image of being a little old fashioned, an image they maintain is no longer valid. It is therefore hoped the rating system will make potential customers more willing and confident to stay in a hostel.

It is necessary for Danhostel to differentiate themselves in the overnight accommodation market. Today there are many competitors fighting for the same customer segment Danhostel caters to. The group cannot compete on pricing because of its competitors' greater financial clout – and the price for overnight accommodation in a hostel is already at rock bottom.

So it's crucial for Danhostel to create a great experience – budget pricing alone is not good enough. Sure, customers are price-conscious, but if they don't have a good experience during their stay, they won't return.

For Danhostel, it is important that a guest's stay at a hostel is experienced as flexible, informal and comfortable.

Customer service means a lot – but not in a traditional

sense. Within the hostels themselves, there is no room service. Good service is, however, synonymous with friendly hosts, a welcoming atmosphere, staff that know the local area and opportunities for children to play.

Even though the hostels can't offer guests a multitude of facilities, the guests are happy with this more personalised form of service.

Danhostel's management naturally has a good grasp of which values the group needs to promote. But

"My guess for the future is that it is better to be a three-star hotel or hostel with a top rating than a five-star hostel with a bad rating."

ultimately it's the customers who determine whether or not the brand lives up to its own values.

Customer loyalty at eye level

It's a common belief that only large corporations, with employees known by prestigious titles such as "customer ambassador" or "manager for customer loyalty", can work seriously with customer loyalty. So let me give you an example of a company with only a few employees – without the fancy titles: Danhostel Copenhagen.

A couple of weeks ago, I visited the hostel and spoke with its manager Lasse Uldahl Borch. I can say with confidence that many customer managers – including those of large corporations – would envy this hostel.

Lasse and his team really have hands-on experience with customer loyalty on a daily basis.

All guests staying at the hostel are offered the chance to participate in an online satisfaction survey. The results of the evaluations are positioned prominently on a large board in an area frequently passed through by staff.

This is truly "customer loyalty at eye level", because staff can't avoid being kept up-to-date.

In addition, the results of the customer satisfaction surveys are discussed at regular team meetings to ensure that the guests' experiences of the hostel constantly continue to improve.

These efforts have paid off: only 144 hostels in the world have achieved a HI-Q-certification as this hostel has done.

Where there's a will there's a way, and all companies that aspire to improve their customer loyalty have the potential to make it.

" It is true that we had some aspirations in terms of the values we wanted to associate with our brand, but ultimately it's the customers who decide if those values really exist. "

NIRAS is Denmark's third largest engineering consultancy company. Within the company, 1,400 specialists and project managers work on projects as diverse as construction and infrastructure, water supply, environment and nature, energy, geodata and development aid. The projects are implemented and completed from more than twenty countries.

NIRAS' project manager, Bjørn Eliasen, relates his experiences of implementing a real-time customer feedback system:

"The challenge was to implement a customer feedback system that gets all our customers to respond to how satisfied they are in our services. We want to be measured on our performance so that we can use the customer feedback as a management tool. Before this, we were only asking a select number of customers about their experiences of being a NIRAS customer. We wanted to do better.

"We had no desire to develop our own survey system. We chose a system that was easy to integrate. That meant that implementing the new system was just a small job for me.

"Our new survey solution gives us the opportunity to compare customer feedback from various business units; however, the aim of comparing customer feedback was not to expose any of our employees as particularly good or bad. On the contrary, we use the customer feedback pro-actively in our partnership with them. Customer feedback can be a great opportunity to speak to them about what they like about us and how we can improve.

It's great to work with customer satisfaction

"At NIRAS, we believe that it is great to work consistently with customer satisfaction. It is our expectation that, by making customers happy, they will reward us with more orders, while customer feedback helps us improve. NIRAS has always been a customer-orientated company. We have defined business values that we try to achieve: We listen, we learn, we deliver. When we take on a project, then we do so very much on the customer's terms, so we have a corporate culture that revolves around creating customer satisfaction. But we want to do even better."

" We listen,
we learn,
we deliver. **"**

CAD & THE DANDY

Cad & The Dandy – suits with extra service

Cad & The Dandy is a retail chain in London that measures, benchmarks and improves performance among staff through real-time customer feedback. They want customers to be not only satisfied, but so pleased that they become promoters who are willing to recommend Cad & The Dandy to others.

Cad & The Dandy are tailors and shirt-makers based in London and New York. The company has succeeded in expanding rapidly during its first five years. The business model is to make fantastic bespoke suits at fantastic prices. Customer satisfaction plays a big role. Everyone one wants a suit that is tailored in a unique way – it is not a standard product. That is why Cad & The Dandy focuses on their customers as unique individuals.

"Our customers love to look smart – but maybe they don't always shout loud enough about their wishes."

That is why the feedback system is a big asset to the company. Customers can respond to the product and the service they received, for example, "I thought the service was fantastic, but next time I'd appreciate a wider selection to choose from."

This ensures that the top quality of the company's products and services reflect Cad & The Dandy's corporate values.

The company is very conscious of the fact the retail sector is under pressure at the moment, and that luxury products are typically hit the hardest when people tighten their wallets during a recession.

That is why it is necessary for the company to ensure that business is kept on an even keel – despite achieving an increase in revenue of 65 per cent last year.

Cad & The Dandy's business success is based on products and services. The company does not advertise, but instead relies on word of mouth and customer recommendations.

Fundamentally, you need to ensure customers are happy and that your company is offering a perfect service; therefore, when customers evaluate the company, they should never be asked only if they are satisfied – they need to be asked if they would recommend the company to others.

Recommendations are ultimately the reason for Cad & The Dandy's survival and success, the company claims.

" We never advertise; it is simply not worth it. What actually works is recommendations from customers. **"**

Virgin Media has done extremely well in its work to maximise customer loyalty, and they have seen a 35-point increase in their frontline NPS over the past 18 months.

Here is what they did:

Virgin Media taught themselves to really embody the programme, for example, calling dissatisfied customers and closing the loop. They really integrated the whole process into the entire organisation to improve their NPS.

"Okay, over the past three months, how many loops have we closed, and what has been the result of that?"

Everyone in the organisation had a sincere motivation and had his/her own clear goals.

The CEO had a dashboard he would frequently check to monitor the level of customer loyalty – really having his finger on the pulse – for example, the procedure for closing the loop to the customer. Using real-time transactions with NPS, they were able to cover all the critical touchpoints in a typical customer lifecycle.

They had the perspective of the customer journey and the motivation to create a great case story – there is nothing like a good case story to motivate people and get them excited. A metric like NPS can be a little sterile, so it was important to get some great messages communicated to the rest of the organisation so staff felt they were making a difference.

They improved their NPS and their touchpoints significantly as a direct result of being committed to the programme and having everyone engaged in it. It was a big motivator in making a difference in transforming their corporate culture.

During the first eighteen months, they increased the revenue of the organisation and significantly reduced the number of customers who were jumping ship (from 1.8 per cent to 1.1 per cent). This is a significant improvement in churn rate. When they started out, they had among the worst churn rate ever which created many challenges, and they simply had to find a solution.

They actually discovered that those customers who were slamming them with a zero on the 0-10 scale were seventeen times more likely to abandon them than a detractor who had given a different score. Of course, they couldn't prevent everyone from leaving, but segmenting the scale and implementing a strategy of prevention was a key point of their analysis.

And that is what we call a customer journey. They implemented NPS surveys through which they could track the NPS down to the frontline team level and make them responsible for the score. They made it a part of the frontline scorecard and rewarded them for getting 10s. They had all the touchpoints in place to enable them to follow the customer's journey and conditions.

You need to equip the frontline with some diagnostic tools – not complicated diagnostics, but something simple that can be understood relatively quickly. That is day one. That is the day when a customer buys something from Virgin Media. You get the product installed in your home and then you receive your first bill depending on when the installation is made.

And if you're able to measure the NPS of your customer database while you progress through the customer journey, it will help frontline staff to understand where the top and bottom of the scale is and where there is potentially success as well as the less good experiences.

Something else that is important is to have a clear tactical and strategic method for closing the loop to the customer, all the way from the top management to the frontline of the company. The feedback and information that comes from NPS can be used by everyone in the company, if they need it.

The different levels in the company have an internal strategy of how to close the loop on the customer. Team leader interviews with the front line, webinars every month, dashboards, face-to-face meetings with customers, perhaps inviting the customer into your organisation, having a customer committee within management to monitor what is happening in other areas of the organisation. These are all tactical ways of closing the loop to the customers. The strategic way is a little different and has a different process – it is more about investments, etc. Train your organisation to understand the value of NPS.

One of the activities that Virgin Media attempted was having a website dedicated to the strategy. This was a strategic way of closing the loop on the customer because the site was available to everyone. It was not directed at a single person, but they actually said: "Look, we've listened to what you've said. We understand that there have been some problems with the bill, but now we've sorted it all out. We would like to get back to you to tell what it is we've done."

It is far better to honest and upfront with your customers, even when it's not going well, than not communicating with them at all. This is an example of how you build trust with them. You respond to them. They pay to buy something from you – a product or service – so you owe it to them to respond and tell them why they have not received full value for money.

You are ethically obligated to do it.

Richard Branson talks about customer service

It's always insightful to listen to what the boss of the Virgin group, Richard Branson, has to say – and it is always entertaining. Branson recently tweeted this entertaining story from a passenger who wrote a letter of complaint to the company LIAT Airlines:

"Dear LIAT,
May I say how considerate it is of you to enable your passengers such an in-depth and thorough tour of the Caribbean.

Most other airlines I have travelled on would simply wish to take me from point A to B in rather a hurry. I was intrigued that we were allowed to stop at not a lowly one or two but a magnificent six airports yesterday. And who wants to fly on the same airplane the entire time? We got to change and refuel every step of the way!

I particularly enjoyed sampling the security scanners at each and every airport. I find it preposterous that people imagine them all to be the same. And as for being patted down by a variety of islanders, well, I feel as if I've been hugged by most of the Caribbean already.

So thank you, LIAT. I now truly understand why you are The Caribbean Airline.

P.S. Keep the bag. I never liked it anyway."

Branson, posting the story on his blog, wrote that it was wake-up call to companies to focus on what is important for customers:

"Making customer service key to your company will keep your employees motivated and your customers happy. This in turn ensures enduring loyalty, business success and a better experience for everyone."

It is worth noting the strong culture at Virgin and how this creates employees who are exceptionally committed. All the employees get a little package with a motivating message. There is also a book, written by Richard Branson or another entrepreneur. There are stickers saying "Screw it – let's do it" and messages along the lines of, "It's okay to make mistakes, as long as you learn from them." There is a wealth of support and motivation. Virgin really makes an effort to strengthen corporate culture and everyone in the organisation knows it. They invest a lot, not only in NPS, but in working with the corporate culture in general.

These kinds of investments have an overt influence on the culture, which goes well with the NPS programme. For NPS to function, there needs to be a customer-orientated corporate culture.

At Virgin Media, they also have "NPS heroes" – they attempt to make people who did really well into heroes. It is also okay to make mistakes, as long as you learn the lessons from them, and that is exactly what this is: "You can't hide bad experiences – so let's talk about them. It's okay to mess up, but let us instead have a culture in which we talk about it rather than hush it up."

They were very conscious of this, and they arranged annual conferences and big parties. I know that not all companies would do that, but I believe the point is that this is not simply a metric that appears in your reports.

It is not about the metric. This is a programme that creates understanding of the customer experience, and NPS is a way of measuring it. There are other ways to measure, but this really highlights the most important aspects and makes it possible to create change in the culture, which is a central aspect.

66 There are stickers saying 'Screw it – let's do it' and messages along the lines of 'It's okay to make mistakes, as long as you learn from them.' **99**

Summary

- Note that common to all four companies featured above is their approach to customer loyalty: it is more about changing the culture than just measuring and calculating a score.
- Also common to them all is the fact that the measurements are in real time. In this way, you can engage employees so that the customer loyalty strategy becomes an ingrained daily ritual.
- Finally, their measurements are seen as a strong KPI to compare performance over time and to compare their various business units.

PART 2

Stories That
Make a Difference

noma

Not just world-class cuisine

NOMA is known for its world-class cuisine. Its solid reputation has been established by continually pushing the boundaries of what is possible. But this ground-breaking approach didn't just stop with their cuisine. As this story illustrates, NOMA has the same world-class attitude to customer service.

A couple of good friends had had a fantastic evening at NOMA. It was time to pay the bill and a taxi was ordered. They left the restaurant to enter the taxi, and discovered that the taxi meter was already at over $30. When you have just eaten at NOMA, it's not like $30 makes a big difference, but my principled friends thought it was too much. They discussed the matter back and forth with the taxi driver.

Someone from within NOMA witnessed the exchange – an employee, actually. He immediately came out and joined the fray, asking what the problem was. He went back into the restaurant and reappeared, handing the taxi driver the $30 with a big smile, saying, "I hope you all have a really great evening."

How many businesses go that far in offering such amazing service? Does your business go this far? Not many businesses take such a high degree of responsibility for their customers, and most employees certainly would not go that far. This only happens in a business culture in which everyone strives for new levels of excellence – not only product-orientated excellence, but customer service excellence.

 telenor

Great service = great marketing

Some businesses have realised that great service is great marketing. When you provide a great service, you are actually selling the business to the customer. But far too many businesses still see good service as an expense rather than an investment.

Few tell this story better than Tony Evald Clausen, who has worked as a professional salesman for the company The Sales Pilots. He experienced Telenor's excellent service first hand when he contacted them about problems he was having with his Internet. Here is the story as Tony experienced it.

Telenor: "I see that your router is from 2007. We'll send you a new one. Of course, it will cost you nothing; I see that you have been a loyal customer with us all the way back to when we were called CyberCity, so I'll send a new router, which you'll have by Wednesday at the latest – at no cost. You can just discard the old one; we don't need it back."

That in itself is fantastic service – but it didn't end there. "When Wednesday arrived, Telenor called me and said they had tried to deliver the router but that they could see that nobody was home to receive it. They asked if it was possible for me to come home later so they could get it delivered. It was possible, so I drove home and managed to get hold of my router.

"Later that evening, Telenor called again, firstly to ask whether I had received the router and secondly to ask whether I had any questions about installing it. I told them I had not tried it yet, so the Telenor employee asked if he could call later in the evening to check that it was all working correctly.

"I installed the router without any problems and, as promised, Telenor called me again later that evening and asked me whether I was satisfied with the router and that all was functioning well.

"It was great service – but it was also a great sales strategy. Telenor had just sold me Telenor all over again. They proved that they are the broadband providers who deserve my money every single month. So it is well deserved that time after time I retell this story and recommend them."

We don't want satisfied customers

E-conomic is a company that is progressing rapidly. Since the start of 2001, the company has amassed a customer base of more than 167,000 companies and has offices in England, Sweden, Norway, Germany and Spain with 100 employees, all of whom are attempting to make a difference.

Users of the e-conomic system probably don't expect anything special in terms of customer service when they buy a subscription for an accounting programme, but e-conomic have made it their goal to offer great customer service that exceeds expectations. By surprising customers with this experience that goes the extra mile, they not only get satisfied customers, but customers who recommend them to friends and colleagues.

Recently, e-conomic surprised a customer who had just quit her subscription. This business owner had been a customer with e-conomic for three years but her company was struggling with too many expenses so they were forced to save wherever possible. Her accountant had urged her to close the business but she was not able to accept this as an option.

When an e-conomic member heard her story, he offered her a free subscription for the rest of the year. The customer responded, "That's really nice of you, but I don't have a penny!"

He insisted, however, that she was a good customer who deserved great service, so he offered her the subscription free for the rest of the year, saying that he would call again to see whether she wished to continue the subscription or cancel it.

The customer was obviously delighted at how far e-conomic were prepared to go for her.

She is today still a happy customer of e-conomic. Even though she may still need to cancel her subscription before the next payment is required, think for a moment about how many people in her network she has shared the e-conomic experience with.

E-conomic say: "We are there for our customers – not because it makes sense, but because it makes f***ing good sense! We train all of our employees in this way of thinking, as we believe that happy customers are the way forward."

Flipping the overturned kayak

We hear a lot about the economic crisis. But you can also "flip the overturned kayak" by focusing on customer loyalty, as this little story will illustrate. This is a contribution from one of our readers:

"One day, six or seven years ago, my husband and I decided to give kayaking a try. There was a long wait to enrol in a course at the kayak club, but we both wondered how hard it could be and drove out to a shop specialising in kayaks. The owner was a little astonished that we wanted to buy a kayak when we hadn't ever tried it before, and immediately talked us out of it – instead, over a period of three weekends during the high season, he rented us various different kayaks so that we could decide which type we wanted. Finally, we bought two kayaks – and they were the right choices. The twist in the story came a few months later, when we paid a quick visit to the shop, which ended up with the salesman offering to take us out kayaking so that we could improve our technique. As you can imagine, I've told this story quite a few times! And recommended the shop to many kayak enthusiasts."

Thank you to Susanne Lehmann Pagh, team leader at Arwos. A bottle of wine is on its way to you and your husband.

The antagonist

A reader contributed the following story about how badly things can go wrong for a shop – in this case a Danish bicycle shop.

"I have a bicycle that I sometimes use to get to work or when I want to fetch the children from playschool. One day I had the dog with me and it ran into the back wheel, breaking the bike. It was handyman time.

When I wanted to get the gears off the back wheel, I discovered that I need specialised tools so had to make a trip to the local bicycle shop. I brought along the wheel and the gears so that he could see what I needed.

Luckily, he had a little tool you could use to separate the wheel from the gear, and best of all it only cost £7. "Great, I'll take it." But, but, but – unfortunately it didn't fit, which I only discovered when I got home. No problem. Back to the bicycle shop ten minutes later.

Luckily, they had a different size I could have. Now, the correct size of the tool cost £6, £1 cheaper. But when the shop owner discovered the price difference he hurriedly removed the packaging and I didn't get my £1 back. And, even worse, I didn't get an apology for the error, which they had clearly made.

But after the experience with the bicycle shop, I've now told this story to ten-twelve people in the local area and have decided not to purchase there again. It became an expensive £1 for the bicycle shop owner.

Luckily, the dog was fine."

What goes around comes around

We invite our readers to submit more great stories for future editions of this book. Send your stories to info@relationwise.com

We may even ask our artist to illustrate your story.

Conclusion:

First measure, then manage

It's important to apply the correct diagnostic. Of course, we can say, "Listen to this. We have the solution to all your problems." That would be one of the world's biggest lies. We have no idea what your biggest problem is. So if one day someone says they know exactly what you need, ask them, "How do you know that?" Because it all starts with applying the diagnostic. In a hospital, it would be an incompetent doctor who, on your first encounter, gave you handful of tablets and asked you to take them because they worked on most people. You wouldn't accept that. But sometimes we accept it when a consultant comes along and says he knows exactly what we need because he's tried it with many other companies. But just because it was a success for other companies, how can we be sure it will work for us? In reality, it's impossible to know this unless some form of analysis, test or self-evaluation is carried out.

When we ask customers what they need, it is not always the case that they believe what we believe.

Sometimes there is a tendency to think inside out. What is easy for us, what is good for us? There is a saying that if you stand with your head in the machine and your backside out in the market, it's difficult to understand what the customer thinks – and apart from that, the customer doesn't get a very good view of the company!

This is why it is so important that you pick yourself up, get a good overview – and then look at the market. You can help yourself or you can ask for help. And only then can we begin with the treatment.

Companies that build on a foundation of customer loyalty have a far greater chance of making it through wider financial headwinds. Poor performance is a result of tactics like customer fees or giving great offers to new customers and simply expecting existing customers to continue paying existing prices.

How loyal are your customers? How certain are you that your customers will still be there tomorrow? If the answer is "Um...", then it's essential to take action and start measuring it. But also measure correctly. As we have discovered, it could be that customers are "just satisfied" with their purchase. But will they buy again tomorrow?

The distinction between loyalty and satisfaction is essentially that satisfaction is something that has already happened. Loyalty is all about expected future behaviour. "Have you considered recommending us? Have you considered purchasing from us again?" That is what it's all about.

If you would like to find out more, visit
www.relationwise.com

66 First measure,
then manage. 99

There are two old management sayings that state, "You can't manage what you don't measure," and, "If you can't measure it, you can't manage it." Sadly, many fail to see the wisdom in these words.

The next step

Ask your clients the ultimate question, and learn something about them

Relationwise conducts tests for companies that wish to get to know their clients better – and improve their sales.

We launch the survey, distribute it to your clients, collect responses and do the calculations. And then we visit with you and go through the results together.

There is no risk involved on your part – except learning how to make better decisions and improve your figures.

The survey will show you what you clients really appreciate, what they are less happy with, and what they want most from you. This will give you the best odds for creating loyal ambassadors and improving your sales.

Order a client survey

1. Make a list with the names and email addresses of some of your clients.
2. We will take care of the design and distribution of the survey.
3. We present the results at a meeting in your company.

If you want to listen to your clients, challenge status quo and improve your sales, then take the first step today.

Contact us at info@relationwise.com

FAQ

Is our response rate high enough?

Because NPS is only one question and an open comment box, and therefore requires only minimum time for respondents to answer, you can expect a significantly higher response rate than from standard customer surveys.

Because action is taken on behalf of dissatisfied customers, customers will also develop greater interest in responding again in the future – contrary to traditional customer surveys in which the data ends up as a statistic that is not to their immediate benefit.

It is impossible to put an exact figure on the sort of response rate you can expect – there are simply too many variables. However, as a starting point, the response rate should be higher than that obtained in standard surveys, and it will continue to increase.

If you are not satisfied with the response rate, you ought to ask yourself if the customer is engaged enough in your touchpoints. Companies that manage to create an emotional connection to the customer obtain a far higher response rate.

Last but not least: remember that change does not happen just because you receive a 100 per cent response rate. Change happens because you continually receive responses you actively work on, on a daily basis.

"Won't we be asking the customers too often?"

In practical terms, you can't ask customers too often – but you can ask an individual customer too often. Customer surveys are important, but for the individual customer it can become annoying if he has to answer the same thing every time he purchases from you. To avoid this, it is possible to configure technical conditions so the individual customer is asked to respond at the most every third or sixth month.

Whom within the customer's organisation should we be measuring?

It is crucial to know who is the decision-maker and who is influential in the hierarchy.

Additionally, beware that you don't cheat yourself. It's common to calculate an average based on many respondents who were really pleased and a single person who was quite angry. The average can hide the angry respondent – whom we should have reached out to from the start and asked what it was that we did wrong.

If you have more questions for our FAQ section, please send them to info@relationwise.com and we promise to respond to them all.

Contributors to the book

Thank you to:

Per Østergaard Jacobsen

Østergaard Jacobsen is arguably the most knowledgeable person in Denmark when it comes to CRM, customer relations and customer experience. A guest lecturer at Copenhagen Business School, he has expertise in performance management and is the author of *The CRM Handbook,* written in 1999 and one of the world's very first books on the subject. This pioneering book sold more than 50,000 copies and became so popular that it was translated into six languages.

Peter Winther

Peter has worked for over twenty-five years in management, sales and sales development, marketing, media, coaching/training, TQM/Lean and, last but not least, CRM-/CEM and loyalty development and dialogue marketing. Peter is a recognised writer and highly popular lecturer. Peter has helped both large and small businesses, both in Denmark and internationally, with strategy, concept development and implementation.

James Young

James Young is a NPS expert. James has previously worked with Satmetrix, the company that, together with Bain Consulting and Fred Reichheld, developed NPS and the technology behind it. James was the consultant responsible for Satmetrix in Europe. Today he runs his own business which primarily helps larger organisations to implement their programmes.

Sources

The Ultimate Question 2.0: How Net Promoter Companies Thrive in a Customer-Driven World by Rob Markey and Fred Reichheld

The Loyalty Effect: The Hidden Force Behind Growth, Profits, and Lasting Value by Frederick F Reichheld

Harvard Business Review on Increasing Customer Loyalty by Harvard Business Review

Customer Satisfaction is Worthless Customer: Loyalty is Priceless by Jeffrey Gitomer

Increasing the 'meaning quotient' of work by McKinsey & Company

66 For me, NPS is successful when I can go anywhere in the organisation, not just in the marketing or sales side, but product development, in supply management, in IT, and I get an answer to the question, 'What NPS feedback are you taking into account in your improvement plans?' And if people look at me as if I come from a different planet, then I know we are not there. **99**

Gerard Kleisterlee
CEO, *Philips*

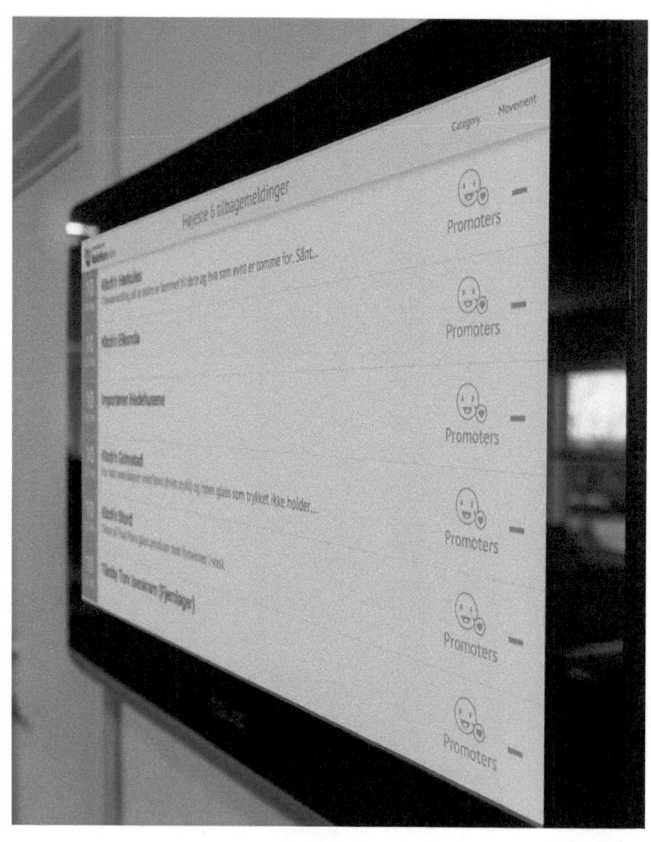

The new piece of furniture in your office

Create a culture that makes your customers and staff say WOW and become a winner in a customer-focussed world.

Working with customer experience and loyalty doesn't need to be all boring reports. We have removed the "dust" and given you our idea of the dashboard of the future, which makes your customer feedback visible across the organisation.

You can only achieve success if you engage your team. When customer feedback is displayed live on a screen in the office, everyone in the company can follow the results. Everyone will feel the success when a customer tells you you've done a good job.

Learn more about the possibilities.
Contact us here info@relationwise.com

Why?

The book Recommended will tell you HOW to get more client ambassadors.

Recommended was followed up by the book Naked Marketing, which is about WHY it is more important today than ever before to redefine your understanding of marketing.

Naked Marketing will teach you that people no longer listen to fancy advertising or smooth salespersons. They speak among themselves – and the future belongs to those companies that give their clients something worth talking about.

Marketing is changing these years from empty advertising to a change-inducing force – and you too can become a change manager.

Download Naked Marketing (PDF file) free of charge at *www.relationwise.com.*

Notes